UNDERSTANDING

FIGURATIVELY SPEAKING

PERSONIFICATION

BY
ROBIN JOHNSON

WITHDRAWN

Crabtree Publishing Company

www.crabtreebooks.com

Crabtree Publishing Company
www.crabtreebooks.com

Author: Robin Johnson

**Publishing plan research
    and development:** Reagan Miller

Photo research: Margaret Amy Salter

Editorial director: Kathy Middleton

Editor: Anastasia Suen

Proofreader and indexer: Wendy Scavuzzo

Cover design and logo: Margaret Amy Salter

**Layout, production coordinator and prepress
    technician:** Margaret Amy Salter

Print coordinator: Margaret Amy Salter

Photographs:
All images by Shutterstock

Personification featured on cover:

Top: the North Wind

Middle left: Death

Middle right: Justice

Bottom center: the Man in the Moon

Bottom right: the Book of Knowledge

Library and Archives Canada Cataloguing in Publication

Johnson, Robin (Robin R.), author
        Understanding personification / Robin Johnson.

(Figuratively speaking)
Includes index.

Issued in print and electronic formats.
ISBN 978-0-7787-1777-5 (bound).--
ISBN 978-0-7787-1877-2 (paperback).--
ISBN 978-1-4271-1618-5 (pdf).--ISBN 978-1-4271-1614-7 (html)

        1. Figures of speech--Juvenile literature. 2. Personification in
literature--Juvenile literature. I. Title.

PN227.J64 2015   j808'.032   C2015-903980-0
                                           C2015-903981-9

Library of Congress Cataloging-in-Publication Data

Johnson, Robin (Robin R.)
 Understanding personification / Robin Johnson.
    pages cm. -- (Figuratively Speaking)
 Includes index.
 ISBN 978-0-7787-1777-5 (reinforced library binding : alk. paper)
 -- ISBN 978-0-7787-1877-2 (pbk. : alk. paper) --
ISBN 978-1-4271-1618-5 (electronic pdf : alk. paper) --
ISBN 978-1-4271-1614-7 (electronic html : alk. paper)
1. Figures of speech--Study and teaching. 2. Personification--Study
and teaching. 3. Figures of speech in literature. 4. Personification in
literature. 5. Discourse analysis, Literary. 6. Style, Literary. I. Title.

 P301.5.F53J64 2015
 808'.032--dc23

                                           2015029464

Crabtree Publishing Company
www.crabtreebooks.com   1-800-387-7650

Printed in Canada/112015/EF20150911

Published in Canada
Crabtree Publishing
616 Welland Ave.
St. Catharines, ON
L2M 5V6

Published in the United States
Crabtree Publishing
PMB 59051
350 Fifth Avenue, 59th Floor
New York, New York 10118

Published in the United Kingdom
Crabtree Publishing
Maritime House
Basin Road North, Hove
BN41 1WR

Published in Australia
Crabtree Publishing
3 Charles Street
Coburg North
VIC, 3058

CONTENTS

WHAT IS PERSONIFICATION?

Buzzzz! Your alarm clock yells at you to wake up. The sun is just starting to poke its head out. The birds are clearing their throats and getting ready to sing. The smell of French toast calls you downstairs for breakfast. *"Viens ici! Come here!"* But your comfy bed begs you to stay just a little while longer. You're barely awake and your day is already packed with **personification**!

Personification is a **figure of speech** in which human **characteristics** or qualities are given to something that is not human. Clocks don't really yell at you to wake up! They just buzz at the time you set the alarm. French toast doesn't really call you for breakfast—in English or French! It just smells so good that it seems as though it is calling you. The sun shines but does not have a head to poke out. Birds sing but don't clear their throats. And beds don't really beg you to stay. They just lie there quietly being beds.

FIGURATIVE OR LITERAL?

We use **literal language** to tell our stories. Literal language states facts or describes things as they really are. We say it is time for the party to start. We don't have time to blow up any more balloons. Those are true statements. Guests will literally be arriving soon!

Personification is a type of **figurative language**. Figurative language uses words or sayings with meanings that are different from their usual literal meanings. We say that time flies when you're having fun. Time does not really fly! It moves at the same pace, minute by minute. We **personify** time to show that it sometimes seems to us to move more quickly, the way a bird flies.

JUST KIDDING!
Why did the girl throw the clock out the window? She wanted to see time fly!

LITERAL
Daniel used a mop to clean the floor.

FIGURATIVE
Daniel and the mop danced across the floor.

WHY USE PERSONIFICATION?

We use personification to make our stories come alive. We can personify ideas, objects, and animals. Giving them human characteristics—such as walking, talking, and feeling—makes our stories interesting and fun to read. Would you rather read about three boys eating porridge or three bears eating porridge? Wouldn't it be boring if the magic mirror on the wall said nothing at all?

Read the sentences below. Some have personification and some do not. Spot the sentences that make ideas, objects, or animals seem human.

The thirsty plant begged for water.

The dry plant needed water.

The stairs made a creaking noise when we climbed them.

The tired old stairs groaned when we stepped on them.

Darkness crept silently upon the town.

The town suddenly got dark.

ABOUT THIS BOOK

This book is divided into sections to help your stories and poems shout with personification.

 **FIGURE IT OUT!** Explains how personification brings different types of writing to life.

TALK ABOUT IT! Shows you how to brainstorm and use tools to start the writing process.

WRITE ABOUT IT! Features samples and tips to help you write your own poems and stories.

NOW IT'S YOUR TURN! Encourages you to practice personification and create original work.

FIVE STEPS TO WRITING

1. *PRE-WRITING:* Brainstorm and jot down all your ideas. Let your mind race!

2. *DRAFTING:* Your first copy might beg to be neater. You can always clean it up later.

3. *REVISING:* Rewrite and improve your work. Make your words leap off the page!

4. *EDITING:* Check for spelling, grammar, and punctuation errors. Look carefully because they may not jump out at you.

5. *PUBLISHING:* Get your good work out there. It will fly off the shelves!

Artists use personification to paint pictures. They personify ideas in their artwork. Look at the pictures below. Each one represents a different idea—time, justice, nature, and the New Year. Study the images carefully, then guess the idea that each picture personifies.

 **FIGURE IT OUT!**

Did you guess which idea is personified in each picture? The text below explains the artwork.

Time is personified as an old man named Father Time. He has a long, flowing beard and an even longer flowing robe. In one hand, Father Time carries a staff or scythe. A scythe is a farming tool used to cut down wheat for harvest. It shows that all living things grow and die over time. In his other hand, Father Time carries an hourglass. An hourglass is a device used to measure time. When the sand in an hourglass runs out, time is up!

The New Year is personified as a bouncing baby boy named Baby New Year. He represents new life and a fresh start to the year. Unlike Father Time, Baby New Year does not wear a robe. In fact, he often wears only a diaper—or nothing at all! He sometimes wears a fancy top hat and looks ready to party. Happy Baby New Year!

Nature is personified as a lovely woman named Mother Nature. She has a kind face and flowers in her hair. She wears a long dress or flowing robe. Mother Nature is always surrounded by plants and animals. Sometimes she holds a globe in her strong but gentle hands. She is also known as Mother Earth.

Justice is personified as a serious woman named Lady Justice. She is blind or blindfolded, because justice should never be affected by how people or events look. Like Mother Nature, Lady Justice wears a long dress or robe. Unlike Mother Nature, Lady Justice is all business. She has no time to frolic with animals or put flowers in her hair. Lady Justice carries weigh scales and a sword. The scales show the balance between right and wrong. The sword shows that criminals will be punished.

Brooke wanted to try to personify an idea. She decided to draw her own picture of Mother Nature. She thought of some characteristics of nature. A characteristic is a feature or quality that identifies a person or thing. Brooke wrote the characteristics in a tree chart.

Rivers and lakes are blue.

Grass and leaves are green.

The sun is round and yellow.

Baby animals and other things grow in nature.

NATURE

Then Brooke considered how she could personify nature in her drawing. Mother Nature could have hair that was yellow to represent the sun. She could be dressed in green to represent the grass and leaves. She could have blue arms and legs that move the way rivers do.

Brooke used her tree chart to write a few sentences about Mother Nature. Then she drew a picture that personified her. She added a baby carriage to make her look like a mother.

Mother Nature is good and kind. She cares for baby animals. She tells the sun to smile down on Earth. The rivers follow behind her as she wanders through the forests. The grass and leaves like to dance for her in the wind.

NOW IT'S YOUR TURN!

Now it's your turn to paint a picture! You can personify nature, time, hope, joy, or any other idea. Make a list of characteristics. Then use the list to personify the idea in words and art.

PERSONIFICATION IN POEMS

Poets use personification to paint pictures with words, too. They use words to bring ideas, objects, and animals to life. The poem below is about a shadow. Which words give the shadow human characteristics?

MY SHADOW

I have a little shadow that goes in and out with me,
And what can be the use of him is more than I can see.
He is very, very like me, from the heels up to the head;
And I see him jump before me, when I jump into my bed.

The funniest thing about him is the way he likes to grow—
Not at all like proper children, which is always very slow;
For he sometimes shoots up taller, like an india-rubber ball,
And he sometimes gets so little that there's none of him at all...

One morning, very early, before the sun was up,
I rose and found the shining dew on every buttercup;
But my lazy little shadow, like [a naughty] sleepy-head,
Had stayed at home behind me and was fast asleep in bed.

—Excerpt from "My Shadow" by Robert Louis Stevenson

FIGURE IT OUT!

The shadow is personified beyond a *shadow* of a doubt! It looks similar to the boy in the poem. In fact, it is very, very like him, "from the heels up to the head." The shadow also acts in similar ways to the boy in the poem. The shadow goes in and out with him, and jumps into bed before him. The shadow could also be personified as an annoying little brother who follows the boy around!

Verbs help bring the shadow to life. In the poem, the shadow goes, jumps, grows, and stays home. Those verbs are normally used to describe the actions of people, not shadows! A child goes to school. A girl jumps up to shoot a basketball. A boy grows too big for his shoes. A sick child stays home from school. Using these verbs helps give the shadow human qualities.

Adjectives in the poem also make the shadow seem human. The poet describes the shadow as little, lazy, and sleepy. Have you ever described an object that way? Maybe some of your toys are little, but they aren't usually described as lazy or sleepy!

The poet uses the **pronouns** "he" and "him" to refer to the shadow. We normally use those pronouns when we talk about males, not shadows! We use the pronoun "it" to refer to a shadow or other object. Using the male pronoun gives the shadow a boyish quality and helps bring it to life.

Owen wanted to practice personification. He decided to personify an everyday object, the way the poet did in "My Shadow." First, he made a list of possible **nouns**. He chose some nouns from the poem. He also thought up some new nouns. Then Owen picked one noun from his list and circled it. It would be the subject of his poem.

NOUNS:

dew

buttercup

(ball)

apple

frog

toothbrush

Next, Owen made a list of verbs. He chose actions that people normally do. He wrote them down in another list. The verbs would help personify the ball in his poem.

VERBS:

grin

sit

twirl

fly

look

sweat

wait

14

Owen used the noun and verbs in his lists to write a short poem. He added some adjectives to help bring the ball to life. He used a female pronoun to personify it even more.

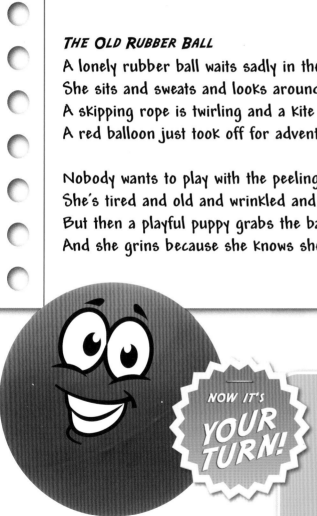

THE OLD RUBBER BALL

A lonely rubber ball waits sadly in the sun.
She sits and sweats and looks around at others having fun.
A skipping rope is twirling and a kite is flying high,
A red balloon just took off for adventure in the sky.

Nobody wants to play with the peeling rubber ball.
She's tired and old and wrinkled and can barely bounce at all.
But then a playful puppy grabs the ball and darts away,
And she grins because she knows she'll have a doggone good old day.

NOW IT'S YOUR TURN!

Now it's your turn to write a poem! Make a list of nouns and choose a subject for your poem. Next, make a list of verbs. Choose actions that people normally do. Add some adjectives. Then put it all together and bring an everyday object to life!

PERSONIFICATION IN FABLES

You have seen that personification helps artists paint pictures and poets write poetry. But did you know that personification is also perfect for **prose**? Prose is spoken or written words told in sentences. Prose is used in **fables**, fairy tales, plays, and novels.

Fables are short stories used to teach **morals**, or lessons. They often include objects and animals that act the same as humans do. Aesop, the writer of this fable, personifies the sun and wind to tell his blustery tale.

THE NORTH WIND AND THE SUN

The North Wind and the Sun had a quarrel about which of them was the stronger. While they were disputing with much heat and bluster, a Traveler passed along the road wrapped in a cloak.

"Let us agree," said the Sun, "that he is the stronger who can strip that Traveler of his cloak." [Whoever gets the man to remove his cloak is the stronger of the two of them.]

"Very well," growled the North Wind, and at once sent a cold, howling blast against the Traveler. With the first gust of wind the ends of the cloak whipped about the Traveler's body. But he immediately wrapped it closely around him, and the harder the Wind blew, the tighter he held it to him. The North Wind tore angrily at the cloak, but all his efforts were in vain.

Then the Sun began to shine. At first his beams were gentle, and in the pleasant warmth after the bitter cold of the North Wind, the Traveler unfastened his cloak and let it hang loosely from his shoulders. The Sun's rays grew warmer and warmer. The man took off his cap and mopped his brow. At last he became so heated that he pulled off his cloak, and, to escape the blazing sunshine, threw himself down in the welcome shade of a tree by the roadside.

Moral: *Gentleness and kind persuasion win where force and bluster fail.*

FIGURE *IT OUT!*

This sunny story shines with personification! There are three **characters** in the fable—the North Wind, the Sun, and a Traveler. The North Wind and the Sun are the stars of the show. They are personified beings with human traits. They talk, boast, and argue about which one is stronger. In fact, the only character without any **dialogue** is the human Traveler!

The North Wind is a cold, tough character. He growls and sends a "cold, howling blast" against the Traveler. He blows harder and harder at the man, tearing angrily at his cloak. We picture the wind's icy fingers tugging at the cloth. But the cold wind only makes the man grip his coat even tighter.

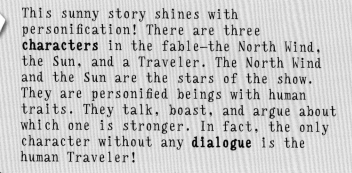

The Sun seems to be a warm, kind character. At first, he shines his beams gently down on the Traveler. The man warms up and unbuttons his heavy cloak. But the Sun does not stop there. His rays grow warmer and warmer. The man removes his hat and mops his brow. Finally, the blazing Sun grows so hot, that the uncomfortable man must take off his cloak and hide from the Sun under a shady tree.

The moral of the story is that gentle persuasion is better than force. But is the Sun really so gentle? He argues and competes with the North Wind. He turns up the heat until the Traveler sweats and gets too hot. The Sun is strong and persistent. He wins the contest—but he may not win any prizes for kindness in this fable.

TALK ABOUT IT!

Mason wanted to write his own fabulous fable. He thought of morals he could teach others. He could tell people to wear sunscreen. After all, he had just learned how strong the sun was! Mason brainstormed other ideas and had lots of food for thought. Finally, he picked a juicy moral—why you should always chew with your mouth closed.

Then Mason thought of objects to personify in his food fable. He could play catch with a tossed salad. He could make a hot potato look cool. He could teach a bad egg to be good. Mason decided to bring a simple sandwich to life. He used a sandwich chart (of course!) to plan his story.

Topic:
SAM IN A JAM

Detail: Sam is making a peanut butter sandwich for lunch.

Detail: The sandwich demands that he add some jelly.

Detail: He chews with his mouth closed to keep the sandwich quiet.

Concluding Sentence or Moral:

It's good manners—and much quieter—to chew with your mouth closed!

Mason used his sandwich chart to make a tasty fable. He added characters and dialogue—but not jelly!—to make it more delicious.

SAM IN A JAM

One day, Sam was making himself a sandwich. He spread some peanut butter on a slice of bread. He was just about to close up the sandwich when he heard a little voice. The sandwich whispered, "I would like some jelly on me, please." Sam leaned in closer to hear the sandwich better. It repeated the same sentence, a bit louder now. "I would like some jelly on me, please."

Sam did not like jelly, so he told the sandwich no. He closed up the bread and cut the sandwich in half. Then he sat down and began to eat his lunch. But the sandwich kept getting louder. "I want jelly," it said in a firm voice. Then it began to shout, "Give me some jelly!"

Sam covered the sandwich so he wouldn't hear it anymore. He took a bite, then quickly covered it up again. But now the sandwich was yelling from inside his mouth! The sentences were chewed up, but the words were loud and clear. "Give... me... some... jelly!"

Then Sam realized he was chewing with his mouth open. He shut his mouth and couldn't hear the rude sandwich at all. So he kept his mouth closed and had a nice quiet lunch.

Moral: It's good manners—and much quieter—to chew with your mouth closed!

NOW IT'S YOUR TURN!

Now it's your turn to come to the fable table! Brainstorm a moral you would like to share. Then think of objects to tell your story. Use stars, sneakers, soup, or anything else. Bring the objects to life and teach the reader a lesson.

PERSONIFICATION IN FAIRY TALES

Fairy tales are full of personification! Fairy tales are short children's stories about magical beings and lands. Some include objects that talk or act like people. A magic mirror tells the evil queen about Snow White's beauty. The Gingerbread Man runs and runs, as fast as he can.

Other fairy tales feature animals that act as though they are humans. The Three Little Pigs build houses made of straw, sticks, and bricks. The Big Bad Wolf dresses up in Granny's clothes to trick Little Red Riding Hood. And Goldilocks discovers the home of three very civilized bears.

THE STORY OF THE THREE BEARS

Once upon a time there were three Bears, who lived together in a house of their own, in a wood. One of them was a Little Wee Bear, and one was a Middle-sized Bear, and the other was a Great Big Bear. They each had a bowl for their porridge... And they each had a chair to sit in... And they each had a bed to sleep in...

One day, after they had made the porridge for their breakfast, and poured it into their porridge-bowls, they walked out into the wood while the porridge was cooling, [so] that they might not burn their mouths by beginning too soon, for they were polite, well-brought-up Bears. And while they were away a little girl called Goldilocks... passed by the house, and looked in at the window. And then she peeped in at the keyhole, for she was not at all a well-brought-up little girl. Then seeing nobody in the house she lifted the latch. The door was not fastened, because the Bears were good Bears, who did nobody any harm, and never suspected that anybody would harm them. So Goldilocks opened the door and went in; and well pleased was she when she saw the porridge on the table. If she had been a well-brought-up little girl she would have waited till the Bears came home, and then, perhaps, they would have asked her to breakfast; for they were good Bears—a little rough or so, as the manner of Bears is, but for all that very good-natured and [welcoming]. But she was an [impolite], rude little girl, and so she set about helping herself.
—Excerpt from "The Story of the Three Bears"
by Flora Annie Steel

20

FIGURE IT OUT!

In this passage, Goldilocks discovers an empty cabin in the woods. She enters it and makes herself right at home! As the story continues, Goldilocks tastes the bears' porridge. One is too hot and one is too cold. But the third bowl is just right, so she eats it up. Then Goldilocks sits in the bears' chairs, and lies down in their beds. When the bears return, they discover that someone has been eating, sitting, and sleeping in their home. Goldilocks wakes up and jumps out a window.

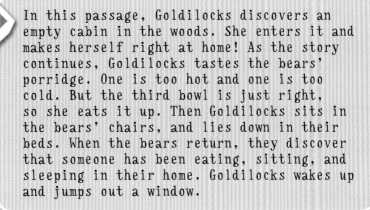

The personified bears in this story are barely bears. They talk, live, and act like people. They own a house (or at least are renting it). So we know they work hard and pay their bills. The bears cook meals and use dishes. They sit on chairs, eat at a table, and sleep in beds. Real bears don't do any of those things!

Personification makes this story interesting. It also makes it **ironic**. The word "ironic" describes something that happens the opposite way than is expected. We know that bears are wild animals. We expect them to live in caves and hunt for food. But in this story, the bears are more civilized than the girl! We think that little girls are sweet and polite. But Goldilocks is not as good as gold! She breaks into a house, steals food, and damages property. This fairy tale teaches us to respect others and that things are not always what they seem.

TALK ABOUT IT!

Noah wondered how "The Story of the Three Bears" would sound with different animals. He imagined Goldilocks and the Three Elephants, but those animals were too big. He pictured Goldilocks and the Three Mice, but those animals were too small. Finally, he imagined Goldilocks and the Three Pigs. Those animals were just right!

Noah knew that people picture pigs as positively sloppy. So he decided to write about some clean pigs with an even cleaner home. Noah used a story map to plan his pig tale. He jotted down notes for the beginning, middle, and end of his story.

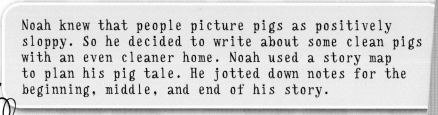

BEGINNING
- Once upon a time, three pigs lived in a nice home.
- They always kept it clean and tidy
- One day, the three pigs went out.

MIDDLE
- While they were gone, a mucky cat snuck in.
- He messed up their home and ate their food.
- Then he fell asleep on the couch.

END
- Arriving home, the pigs saw the mess left by the cat.
- They showed the cat how to clean up his mess.
- Then they all sat down for a nice meal.

Noah added some details to bring his animals to life. He borrowed some characters from other fairy tales, too. Then he put it all together to write his pig tale. He hoped it wouldn't *boar* his friends!

A TALE OF THREE LITTLE PIGS

Once upon a time, three little pigs lived together in a pretty place. They were proud of their home and kept it as neat as a pin. They were always sweeping, mopping, dusting, and scrubbing. One day, the pigs went out to buy some cleaning supplies. While they were gone, a cat named Puss in Boots snuck in through a window. The cat had mud all over his boots! He walked on the tables, chairs, and floor. He tracked mud everywhere! Then the cat raided the cookie jar. He ate all the gingerbread cookies—except the one that ran away. That messy cat got crumbs all over the kitchen! Finally, Puss in Boots curled up on the couch to take a nap. He got cat fur everywhere! When the three pigs returned home, they were shocked to see such a pigsty! But they knew that cats are messy by nature. So they showed the cat how to scrub the mud, wipe up the crumbs, and clean the couch. Then they all sat down for some pancakes.

NOW IT'S YOUR TURN!

Now it's your turn to write a fairy tale. Use "The Story of the Three Bears" as a model or choose your favorite fairy tale. Change the animals and objects in the story. Give them human characteristics. Then make them all live happily ever after.

PERSONIFICATION IN NOVELS

Personification gives us new ways to look at everyday things. It also helps us imagine how something might feel—if it could have feelings! Understanding and sharing the feelings of others is called **empathy**. Empathy is important because it leads to kindness. It's hard to be mean to someone when you put yourself in their shoes.

The novel *Black Beauty* is an **autobiography** of a horse. An autobiography is a true tale you write about yourself. Black Beauty tells his life story and shows us what it's like to be a horse. In this passage, we learn straight from the horse's mouth how it feels to wear a bridle (leather straps around the head) and a metal bit inside the mouth.

I had of course long been used to a halter and a headstall, and to be led about in the fields and lanes quietly, but now I was to have a bit and bridle; my master gave me some oats as usual, and after a good deal of coaxing he got the bit into my mouth, and the bridle fixed, but it was a nasty thing! Those who have never had a bit in their mouths cannot think how bad it feels; a great piece of cold hard steel as thick as a man's finger to be pushed into one's mouth, between one's teeth, and over one's tongue, with the ends coming out at the corner of your mouth, and held fast there by straps over your head, under your throat, round your nose, and under your chin; so that no way in the world can you get rid of the nasty hard thing; it is very bad! yes, very bad! at least I thought so; but I knew my mother always wore one when she went out, and all horses did when they were grown up; and so, what with the nice oats, and what with my master's pats, kind words, and gentle ways, I got to wear my bit and bridle.

—Excerpt from *Black Beauty* by Anna Sewell

FIGURE IT OUT!

The **narrator** of the passage is a horse, of course. A narrator is someone—or something—that tells a story. Most horse stories are told from the rider's point of view. But this horse tale is different. Personifying Black Beauty shows us his point of view and helps us feel empathy for horses. After all, those "who have never had a bit in their mouths cannot think how bad it feels."

Black Beauty describes the bit as a "nasty hard thing." It is "a great piece of cold hard steel as thick as a man's finger" pushed into your mouth and held tightly by straps. Black Beauty does not like wearing the bit one bit, but he knows he has no choice. Have you ever had to wear something you didn't like? Maybe you had glasses that always slid off your nose. Maybe you got braces that hurt your teeth. And maybe only a hug—and some ice cream!—made you feel better.

Horses don't eat ice cream, but they do like oats. Black Beauty's master gives him oats, then coaxes the bit into his mouth. (Remember Aesop's fable taught us that gentle persuasion is better than force.) Black Beauty says, "what with the nice oats, and what with my master's pats, kind words, and gentle ways, I got to wear my bit and bridle." The novel shows us how to treat horses and helps us understand them a little *bit* better.

TALK
ABOUT IT!

Lily wanted to personify an animal. She considered different subjects for her story. She could choose a fly that flies fast or a cow that mooooves slowly. She could pick a shark that snacks a lot or a bat that just hangs around. She decided to write a sweet story about a skunk.

have bushy tails

are small mammals

have black-and-white striped fur

SKUNKS

come out at night

scare people

spray a smelly substance when scared

Lily wrote down everything she knew about skunks. She used a spider map to catch all the facts. She would use those facts to help bring the skunk to life.

WRITE ABOUT IT!

Lily used the chart to write her skunk story. The facts were all there in black and white! She made the skunk the narrator so it would seem more human. She hoped her skunk tale didn't stink!

Why doesn't anyone like me? I have black-and-white fur, and so do zebras. Everyone loves zebras! I have a bushy tail, and so do squirrels. People love squirrels! But when people see me, they scream and run away. That really hurts my feelings! I only come out at night. But I'm a nice girl and I never hurt anyone. In fact, I have some sweet perfume that I share with people and animals I meet. Would you like me to spray some on you?

In the next chapter, you will see how other students made Lily's story even sweeter.

NOW IT'S YOUR TURN!

Now it's your turn to tell an animal tale! Pick a subject for your story. Write down facts about the animal in a spider map. Then put yourself in its shoes—or hoofs—and imagine its story.

REVISE YOUR WORK

You have learned how to brainstorm and write first drafts. You brought ideas, objects, and animals to life. Now you will learn how to revise your work and perfect your personification.

PERSONIFICATION REVISION CHECKLIST

1. Does your story describe an idea, object, or animal?

2. Did you give human characteristics to your non-human subject?

3. Did you include verbs, adjectives, adverbs, and pronouns normally used to describe people?

4. Does personifying your subject help paint a picture and bring it to life?

WORD CHOICE

The words you choose for your stories show the reader your **voice.** Voice is the unique personality of each writer that shows in their word choices. Your word choices also bring your subject to life in different ways. When you change adjectives, verbs, and **adverbs**, you change how people see your subject. Imagine that Lily had used the adjectives "mean" and "smelly" instead of "nice" and "sweet." What kind of picture would that paint? How else could different words personify the skunk in different ways?

WORK TOGETHER

A good way to revise your work is to share it with other students. They will make sure it doesn't stink! Have you given human traits to your non-human subject? Can the students imagine the picture you are trying to paint? The group will also help you spot spelling and grammar errors that snuck past you.

MAKE IT BETTER

Lily shared her skunk story with some other students. They liked her work, but suggested ways to make it even sweeter.

Owen thought she should add some adjectives to her story. He said the words "striped" and "big" would help paint a picture of the skunk. Mason suggested she add a reason why the skunk might come out at night. Saying she was shy would make her more likable. Brooke thought it would be clever to say that people go nuts for squirrels, since squirrels eat nuts.

Lily listened carefully to their suggestions. She agreed that the changes would make her story sound—and smell—better. So she revised her work. Then she helped some other students improve their stories and bring their subjects to life.

Why doesn't anyone like me? I have black-and-white striped fur, and so do zebras. Everyone loves zebras! I have a big bushy tail, and so do squirrels. People go nuts for squirrels! But when people see me, they scream and run away. That really hurts my feelings! I'm a little shy so I only come out at night. But I'm a nice girl and I never hurt anyone. In fact, I have some sweet perfume that I share with people and animals I meet. Would you like me to spray some on you?

PUBLISH YOUR WORK

Now that you have perfected personification, it's time to publish your work. Publishing means getting it ready for an **audience**. An audience is all the people who see, read, or hear your work. Publishing is the final step in the writing process.

There are plenty of ways to publish your personifications. Paint a picture and hang it on your fridge. Write a fable and teach your friends a lesson. Read your tale of three little pigs to your three little brothers. Just keep creating and publishing—and your good work will speak for itself!

30

LEARNING MORE

BOOKS

Aesop's Fables retold by Ann McGovern. Scholastic Inc., 1963.

Black Beauty by Anna Sewell. Penguin Young Readers Group, 2011.

Charlotte's Web by E.B. White. HarperCollins, 2012.

Poetry for Young People: Robert Louis Stevenson by Frances Schoonmaker (ed.). Sterling, 2008.

WEBSITES

Personification Super Shooter Basketball Review Game
http://reviewgamezone.com/games/supershooter/index.php?1635&title=Personification
Answer personification questions and shoot hoops in this fun game.

YouTube: Personification
www.youtube.com/watch?v=RDt1I0R3cdI
A grumpy cat learns about personification in this funny video.

My Word Wizard: Personification Poems
www.mywordwizard.com/personification-poems.html
Visit this website to read some personification poems—then publish your own!

GLOSSARY

Note: Some boldfaced words are defined where they appear in the book.

adjective A word that describes a noun

adverb A word that describes a verb

brainstorm To think of many ideas, often in a group

character A person, animal, or thing that interacts with others in a story

dialogue The things characters say in a story

figure of speech A word or phrase that is not used in the usual or literal way

moral A lesson learned from a story

noun A word that names a person, animal, place, thing, or idea

personify To give human characteristics to an idea, object, or animal

persuasion Actions or words used to try to influence another person's decisions or actions

pronoun A word that takes the place of a noun

verb An action word that tells what a person or thing is doing

voice A writer's personality that shows in their word choices

INDEX